a Jar of Jokes

ISBN 0 3303 5830 8

Published in Australia 1996 by Pancake
an imprint of Pan Macmillan Australia Pty. Ltd.
St. Martins Tower, 31 Market Street
Sydney NSW 2000

Printed in Hong Kong by South China Printing Co.(1988) Ltd.
Reprinted 1997, 1998 (three times), 1999 (twice), 2000 (twice),
2001 (three times)

© Pancake

All rights reserved

If ten birds were sitting on a branch and you shot one, how many would be left?
None. They would all fly away.

If twelve make a dozen, how many make a million?
Very few.

What weighs three tons, has tusks, and loves pepperoni pizza?
An Italian circus elephant.

What did one wig say to the other?
"I love you so much I'd even curl up and dye for you".

What has spots, weighs four tonnes, and loves peanuts?
An elephant with the measles.

What is big, likes peanuts, and has a trunk?
An oak tree with a squirrel in it.

What is green and pecks on trees?
Woody Wood Pickle.

What do you call a hot-dog who always speaks his mind?
A frank-furter.

Why do tigers have stripes?
Because they'd look funny in polka dots.

What has two feet, a high-powered rifle, and spots before its eyes?
A hunter shooting at a leopard.

What did the surgeon say to the patient?
"Suture self."

What is pear-shaped, yellowish-red, and costs six million dollars?
The Bionic Mango.

Why can't you trust comedians?
Because they're always pulling some kind of funny business.

When Hawaiians play basketball, what do they use for nets?
Hula Hoops.

Why do birds fly south for the winter?
Because they can't afford to take the train.

What did Cinderella Fish wear to the ball?
Glass Flippers.

What game do mother hens play with their babies?
Peck-a-boo.

Why does Uncle Sam wear red, white and blue braces?
To hold up his trousers.

What's grey, has very large ears, four legs and a trunk?
A mouse taking a sea voyage.

If you see ten little tomatoes all in a row, which one is the cowboy?
None. They're all redskins.

What's the longest word in the dictionary?
Smiles. There's a mile between the first and last letter.

Why did Robin Hood only rob the rich?
Because the poor had no money.

What's the difference between a hill and a pill?
One is hard to get up and the other is hard to get down.

Name two things you can never eat before breakfast.
Lunch and dinner.

A doctor, a lawyer, and a chicken inspector are all walking down the street together. Which one wears the largest hat?
The one with the largest head.

What did the waterfall say to the water fountain?
"You're nothing but a little squirt."

Why do kettles whistle?
Because they never learned to sing.

Which fruit is always sad?
Blueberries.

Where can you always find a helping hand?
At the end of your arm.

What kind of paper do you use to make a kite?
Fly paper, of course.

What do you get when a herd of elephants stampede though a field of corn and beans?
Succotash.

What's the difference between a tiny elephant and a gigantic mouse?
About 1500 kilograms.

What happens to two frogs who try to catch the same insect at the same time?
They end up tongue-tied.

Why did the father call his son Bulb?
Because the boy was the light of his life.

What would you call a cow that sits on the grass?
Two hundred kilos of ground beef.

What did the optician say to his glasses?
"Stop making spectacles of yourselves."

What time is it when an elephant climbs into your bed?
Time to get a new bed.

Why is a tennis court so noisy?
Because every player on it raises a racket.

What is the fastest way to go to the hospital?
Pick a fight with an elephant.

What does a polite mouse always say?
"Cheese and thank you".

Why did the corn go to the doctor's office?
Because it had an earache.

What's the best way to come face to face with a timid mouse?
Lie down in front of a mouse hole and cover your nose with cheese spread.

What's the best way to get a rhino's attention?
Honk his horn.

What has wings, smokes, and walks on ceilings?
A fire breathing dragonfly.

What do termites eat for dessert?
Toothpicks.

What is the easiest thing for a trapper to catch in a tropical rain forest?
A cold.

Why is a king like a summer shower?
Because they both reign. (rain)

When does a dandelion look shabby?
When it's going to seed.

What do diets and promises have in common?
They're always being broken.

What do you call an Asian ox that talks a lot?
A Yakety-Yak!

Where do geologists go to have a good time?
To Rock Festivals.

What should you save for a rainy day?
Your umbrella.

What always goes up in smoke?
A fire.

What's easier to give than to receive?
Criticism.

Why was the hockey player successful?
Because he always kept his goals in mind.

What American city is a name for a sandy place with tropical trees?
Palm Beach.

What was the name of the skunk who painted the Mona Lisa?
Leonardo DaStinki.

Generals pin medals on heroes. What do they pin on traitors?
The blame.

Why is an ear of corn like the officer's dining room in the army?
Because they are both full of kernels. (colonels)

What Arizona city is a name for a flag pole?
Flagstaff.

What American city is a name for a body of water containing sodium chloride?
Salt Lake City.

What do you find inside Beagle puppies?
Dog bones.

What's stingy, hates Christmas, and lays eggs?
Ebenezer Chicken.

Why did the boy put on wet trousers?
Because the tag said, "Wash and Wear."

Why can't a banana stay in the sun too long?
Because a banana peels.

What kind of gum do bees make?
Bumble gum.

Who carries a basket, visits Grandma, and steals jewellery?
Little Red Robin Hood.

What is brilliantly intelligent, weighs 90 kilograms, and is made out of iron?
Albert Einstein Dumbbell.

What do you call a store that sells only the books of Samuel L. Clemens?
A Twain station.

What's red, white and blue, and handy if you sneeze?
Hankie Doodle Dandy.

Who's white, has two eyes made out of coal, and can't move fast?
Frosty the Slowman.

What's spiral in shape and very crowded?
A snail with a houseguest.

Who flies through the air and calls the kettle black?
Peter Pot.

What builds dams in a stream and is very, very dangerous?
A beaver with a cleaver.

Who screams, "The sky is falling! The sky is falling!" and suffers from inflation?
Henny Tenpence.

What's bright red, goes screeching down the street, and has lots of little cones?
A fire engine that sells ice cream.

What's made out of tin and circles the earth?
The can in the moon.

What has brown fur, wears a ranger's hat, and hangs from a tree?
Smokey the Pear.

What lives in a barn, has wool, and always has something to keep its hands busy?
A sheep who knows how to knit.

What's faster than a speeding bullet, more powerful than a locomotive, able to leap tall buildings in a single bound, and has a car park?
Super Market.

What weighs 200 kilos, moves its legs in a circle, and has wheels?
A fat lady on a bicycle.

What's 96 years old, walks with a stick, and wears three fur coats?
A little cold lady.

What do you get if you cross a flying insect with indigestion?
A rumblebee.

Who lives in a bog and casts magical spells?
The Wizard of Ooze.

What barks, saves people in trouble, and is made out of kitchen foil?
Rin-Tin-Aluminium.

Who catches crooks and wears frilly clothes?
Dick Lacy.

Who has seven eyes, lives underground, and conquered the world?
Alexander the Potato.

Who rides in a sleigh, gives Christmas presents, and has many faults?
Santa Flaws.

What's blue, carries a truncheon, and bounces?
A rubber policeman.

What has a long tail, eats bananas, and disappears four hours every day?
A monkey with a part-time job.

Who invented the telephone and is delicious with milk?
Alexander Graham Cracker.

Who rides on a raft, hates school, and hardly ever eats?
Huckleberry Thin.

What has seeds, a stem, and swings from tree to tree?
Tarzan of the Grapes.

What do you get if you cross a song without words, with a quick snack?
A humburger.

What do you get if you cross an American pioneer with a game?
Davy Cricket.

What's covered with suds and sings high C's?
The soprano in a soap opera.

What's green, sour, and sings in old movies?
Jeanette MacPickle.

What's shaped like a bell and climbs up the side of the Empire State Building?
King Bong.

Who has to be very, very careful in the cow barn?
A milkmaid with cold hands.

What grows on a tree and is terrified of wolves?
The Three Little Figs.

Who can hit high C twelve times in a row without taking a breath?
A soprano with the hiccups.

What do you get if you cross a flying machine with a policeman?
A Helicopper.

Who does the bunny hop in its sleep?
A sleeping rabbit with the hiccups.

What is large and grey and bumps into submarines?
A short-sighted hippo scuba diver.

What does a 200 kilo parrot say?
"Polly wants a cracker NOW!"

What did the road say to the bridge?
"You make me cross."

What kind of bird eats the same worm eight times?
A swallow with the hiccups.

Why does the stork stand on one foot?
Because if he lifted the other, he'd fall down.

What's the difference between the mumps and the measles?
With the mumps you shut up, and with the measles you break out.

If you were locked in a room with only a piano, how would you get out?
Play the piano until you find the right key.

What did the boy say when he found a button in his salad?
"I guess it fell off when the salad was dressing."

What do you give others and still keep yourself?
A cold.

What kind of dog says, "Meow"?
A police dog in disguise.

What bus crossed the ocean?
Columbus.

What's a wooden wedding?
When two Poles get married.

Why did the hippo stop using soap?
Because he left a ring around the river.

Why did the elephant have holes in his hide?
Because he forgot to put moth balls in his trunk.

In a young boy, what's cleanliness next to?
Impossible.

What colour do you paint a guitar?
Plink.

What do you use when a tree has a puncture?
A lumberjack.

Why does a bald-headed man have no use for keys?
Because he's lost his locks.

Why is a moth's life so terrible?
Because it spends the summer in a fur coat and the winter in a swimming costume.

What do you get if you cross a Brontosaurus with a koala?
An Australian dinosaur that only eats eucalyptus trees.

What do you get if you cross a Tyrannosaurus Rex with a cow?
A monster that eats anyone who tries to milk it.

What do you get if you cross a fire-breathing monster and a flower?
A fire-breathing snapdragon.

What do you get if you cross Bambi with a ghost?
Bamboo.

What do you get if you cross a Brontosaurus with a kangaroo?
A monster that causes earthquakes whenever it hops.

What do you get if you cross a vampire with a Volkswagen?
A thing that attacks luxury cars and sucks out their petrol and oil.

What do you get if you cross the Frankenstein monster with a hot dog?
Frankenfurterstein.

What do you get when you cross a vampire with a dwarf?
A monster that sucks blood out of people's kneecaps.

What do you get if you cross a termite with a Brontosaurus?
A bug that eats the Empire State building for breakfast.

What do you get if you cross a Brontosaurus with a werewolf?
I don't know, but I wouldn't want to be within five hundred miles of it when the moon is full.

What do you get if you cross Santa Claus with a vampire?
A bat that flies down chimneys on Christmas Eve and sucks the sap out of Christmas trees.

What do you get when you cross peanut butter, bread, and a werewolf?
A peanut butter sandwich that gets hairy when the full moon rises.

What's the difference between a thief and a church bell?
One steals from the people. The other peals from the steeple.

What has eyes, but can't see?
A potato.

What has legs, but can't walk?
A bed.

What has three feet, but no toes?
A yardstick.

What has hands and a face, but can't touch or smile?
A clock.

What works only when it's fired?
A rocket.

What has teeth, but no mouth?
A comb.

What has wings, but can't fly?
A mansion.

What has leaves, but is not a plant?
A table.

What looks empty when full?
A balloon.

What has sixteen legs?
Four rabbits.

What is at the end of everything?
The letter g.

What colours would you paint the sun and the wind?
The sun rose and the wind blue.

What pets make exciting music?
Trum-pets.

What does the envelope say when you lick it?
It just shuts up and says nothing.

How can you make paint hurt?
Take out the T.

Why did it take three big boy scouts to help the little old lady cross the street?
Because she didn't want to go.

What has a mouth, but no teeth?
A river.

What has ears, but can't hear?
Corn.

What has arms, but no hands?
A chair.

When fish swim in schools, who helps out the teacher?
The herring aid.

Why do chickens never get rich?
Because they work for chicken feed.

What do vultures always have for dinner?
Leftovers.

What do patriotic American monkeys wave on Flag day?
Star spangled bananas.

How many hot dogs can you eat on an empty stomach?
Only one, because after that your stomach is no longer empty.

Why is it bad to write a letter on an empty stomach?
Because it's much better to write on paper.

Who can marry many a wife and still remain single all of his life?
A minister.

What do you take off last before getting into bed?
Your feet off the floor.

What is everyone in the world doing at the same time?
Growing older.

Why isn't your nose twelve inches long?
Because then it would be a foot.

When are your eyes not eyes?
When the wind makes them water.

When is the end of the world?
After the letter L.

What kind of crew does a ghost ship have?
A skeleton crew.

Why is paper money more valuable than coins?
When you put it in your pocket you double it.
When you take it out it's in creases.

What's the difference between a jeweller and a jailer?
One sells watches, while the other watches cells.

What goes 99-clump, 99-clump, 99-clump?
A centipede with a wooden leg.

Which burns longer, the candles on a girl's birthday cake, or the candles on a boy's birthday cake?
Neither. They both burn shorter.

Why is a baseball game like a pancake?
Because they both depend on the batter.

Teacher: Sylvester, what's the definition of ignorance?
Sylvester: I don't know.

Teacher: Joey, your behaviour is terrible! How many more times am I going to have to keep you in after school?
Joey: 97.
Teacher: 97?
Joey: Yeah. That's how many days are left until the summer holiday.

Teacher: Lucy, where are you going on your summer holiday?
Lucy: Iceland.
Teacher: That's interesting. Why did you choose Iceland?
Lucy: We want to see it before it melts.

Teacher: Everybody knows that Alexander Graham Bell invented the telephone. Stacy, what did his assistant, Mr. Watson do?
Stacy: He sent out the phone bills.

Teacher: Nancy, describe the Battle of the Bulge.
Nancy: My mother when she goes on a diet.

Teacher: Brenda, why don't you want to come on our field trip to study insects?
Brenda: Because they bug me.

Teacher: Mark, what's the one way a person can show that he's a good loser?
Mark: By not punching the winner on the nose.

Teacher: Patrick, you should know the answer to this one... What happens to a person when he kisses the Blarney Stone?
Patrick: He gets cold, dirty lips.

Teacher: Jose, when was the great depression?
Jose: Last week when I got my school report.

Teacher: Zeke, what, besides a supersonic jet, goes faster than the speed of sound?
Zeke: My Aunt Gladys when she talks.

When is the King of Beasts a dandelion?
When he wears a dress suit.

What is a crazy chicken?
A cuckoo cluck.

What do you call a singer who's not old enough to be a tenor?
A niner.

Which kind of policemen play tennis?
Members of the racket squad.

What happened to the boy bee who fell in love?
He got stuck on his honey.

Who is the strongest man in the city?
A traffic cop. He can stop a speeding truck with one hand.

When angels go fishing, what do they catch?
Holy mackerels.

What do you call a small razor?
A little shaver.

Who was the straightest man in the Bible?
Joseph, because Pharaoh made a ruler out of him.

What's the best way to catch a monkey?
Climb a tree and act like a banana.

What is white, lives in the Himalayas, and lays eggs?
The Abominable Snow Chicken.

What do you call a sleeping boy-steer
A bull-dozer.

At what time did God create Adam?
A little before Eve.

What does a leg wear to keep warm?
A knee cap.

Which bird never becomes an adult?
A myna bird.

What's the theme song of Eskimo entertainers?
"There's No Business Like Snow Business."

What wears nine gloves, eighteen shoes, and a mask all at the same time?
A baseball team.

Who wears fifty pairs of socks when it's cold outside?
A centipede.

What happens when gold is left in the open air?
Somebody steals it.

What is big and hairy, wears a dress, and climbs up the Empire State Building?
Queen Kong.

What goes, "Ouch, ouch, ouch, ouch, ouch, ouch, ouch!" when it walks?
An octopus wearing tight shoes.

Who wears a crown, lives in a delicatessen and calls for his fiddlers three?
Old Cole Slaw.

Why did the spy call an exterminator?
Because he thought his room was full of bugs.

What do you call a handsome rabbit who dates a lot of girls?
A Playboy Bunny.

What do you call a vet with laryngitis?
A hoarse doctor.

How can you stop a skunk from smelling?
Put a clothes peg on his nose.

What has seventy-five pairs of sneakers, a ball, and two hoops?
A centipede basketball team.

Why do elephants never get rich?
Because they work for peanuts.

When do kangaroos celebrate their birthdays?
During Leap Year.

What shoes are made for lazy people?
Loafers.

What did one bee say to her nosey neighbour bee?
"Mind your own bee's wax."

What do you do with a mouse that squeaks?
You oil him.

How do you keep a hippopotamus from running away when you take him for a walk?
You tie a hypotenuse around his neck.

Who was the first deer astronaut?
Buck Rogers.

Where does a pig go to pawn his watch?
He goes to a ham hock shop.

What happens when a chimp twists his ankle?
He gets a monkey wrench.

What looks like a dog, has spots, and snickers?
A laughing hyena with a poor sense of humour.

Why did the termite eat balsa wood?
Because he had stomach trouble, and his doctor put him on a soft diet.

What lives in the forest, puts out fires, and has eight arms?
Smokey the Octopus.

How did the tom cat find out he was a father?
His wife sent him a litter.

Why don't exorcists have any friends?
Because they scare the devil out of people.

What did the alien gas man say to the earthling?
"Take me to your meter."

What's the best way to hit a golf ball?
With a golf club.

Why do giraffes find it difficult to apologise?
It takes them a long time to swallow their pride.

How much do used batteries cost?
Nothing, they're free of charge.

What do you get if you feed a chilli pepper to a poodle?
A hot dog.

Why is it easy to play pranks on fish?
Because they always fall for them hook, line and sinker.

Why do fleas never get cold?
Because they're always in fur coats.

Why did the window go to the hospital?
Because it had panes in its sides.

Little boys join the Cub Scouts.
Little girls join the Brownies.
What do little dolphins join?
The Buoy Scouts.

What do you get when you graduate from the Police Academy?
The third degree.

Why is noon like the letter "a"?
Both are in the middle of day.

What's the difference between a crazy rabbit and a counterfeit $10 note?
One is a mad bunny, and the other is bad money.

When is a shaggy dog most likely to enter a house?
When the door is left open.

Where does a general keep his armies?
In his sleevies.

What do alligators wear on their feet?
Alligator shoes.

Who is faster than a locomotive, more powerful than a speeding bullet, and can leap over a tall poodle in a single bound?
Super Flea.

Why is a clock a shy piece of furniture?
Because it covers its face with its hands.

Why should you never invite termites to dinner?
Because they'll eat you out of house and home.

Why are auctioneers the most obedient men in the world?
Because they listen to everyone's bidding.

Who was born on a mountain top, killed a bear when he was only three, and swims underwater?
Davy Crocodile.

What's hairy, rules England, and loves bananas?
King Henry the Ape.

What do Eskimos buy at Christmas time?
Christmas seals.

What does a draughtsman have in common with a fisherman?
They are both anglers.

Why is your secret safe with an egotist?
Because they never talk about anybody but themselves.

You can't buy it in a shop. It's delivered to your house, and you use it every day. What is it?
Electricity.

What could cause you a lot of trouble if it ever stopped smoking?
A chimney.

What do you get if you cross a ham and a karate expert?
Pork chops.

What do you get if you cross a pig and a cactus?
A porkerpine.

What do you get if you cross a kitten and a sapling?
A pussy willow.

What do you get if you cross a poodle with a cuckoo clock?
A watch dog.

What do you get if you cross an envelope with a homing pigeon?
A letter that comes back to you every time you mail it.

What do you get if you cross an elephant with a spider?
I don't know, but when it crawls on your ceiling, the roof collapses!

What do you get if you cross a man-eating tiger and a dog?
An animal that eats people and buries their bones.

What do you get if you cross Satan with a pig?
Devilled ham.

What do you get if you cross two insects and a rabbit?
Bugs Bunny.

What do you get if you cross a pig with a porcupine?
Bacon and pegs.

What do you get if you cross an elephant and a cactus?
The biggest porcupine in the world.

What do you get if you cross a steer and Niagara Falls?
A water buffalo.

What do you get if you cross a frog with an elephant?
An animal that makes a hog of himself at Christmas.

What do you get if you cross an elephant with a swift football striker?
I don't know, but it sure scores a lot of goals.

What do you get if you cross a cat with a cactus?
An animal that gives you a pain whenever it rubs against your leg.

What's the favourite meal of nuclear scientists?
Fission Chips.

What pear can't you eat?
A pair of shoes.

What's worse than finding a maggot in your apple?
Finding half a maggot.

What's yellow and dangerous?
A banana with a machine gun.

Why did the tomato blush?
Because it saw the salad dressing.

What animals in Noah's Ark didn't come in pairs?
Worms, they came in apples.

What do you get when you cross an orange and a squash court?
Orange squash.

How do you remove a peanut from your ear?
Pour chocolate in it; it will come out a treat.

When are the streets greasiest?
When the rain is dripping.

What room has no floor or ceiling, windows or doors?
A mushroom.

What is the main ingredient of dog biscuits?
Collie-flour.

Which fish sleeps a lot?
A kipper.

Why do elephants paint their feet yellow?
So they can hide upside down in custard.

When do elephants paint their toe-nails red?
When they want to hide in strawberry jam.

What do you do if you find a blue banana?
Cheer it up.

What did the cannibal have for lunch?
Baked beings on toast.

A cannibal came home to find his wife cutting up a small native and a boa constrictor.
"Oh no," he said, "not snake and pygmy pie again!"

What did the hamburger say to the tomato?
"That's enough of your sauce."

What do scientists eat?
Microchips.

Why do idiots eat biscuits?
Because they're crackers.

"We had my Granny for Christmas dinner last year."
"Oh? We had turkey."

What do frogs drink?
Croaka Cola.

What do cannibal guests eat for lunch?
Buttered host.

What did the lion say when it saw two hunters in a jeep?
"Hooray! It's meals on wheels."

How do you stop meatballs from drowning?
Put them in gravy boats.

What do jelly babies wear on their feet?
Gum boots.

Why did the cat eat the cheese?
So it could blow down the mouse hole with baited breath.

What did the astronaut see in his frying pan?
An unidentified frying object.

Why was Captain Cook buried in Tahiti?
Because he was dead.

Why do bees have sticky hair?
Because they have honey combs.

Why did the man cross a chicken with an octopus?
So all his family could have a leg each.

What's Chinese and deadly?
Chop Sueycide.

What do you get if you cross a pig with a zebra?
Striped sausages.

What did one strawberry say to the other strawberry?
Between you and me, we shouldn't have got into this jam.

Why did the apple turnover?
Because it saw the swiss roll.

What do you call a man who steals cattle?
A beefburglar.

How do you stop a cock from crowing on Sunday?
Eat it on Saturday.

"This loaf is nice and warm."
"It should be — the cat's been sitting on it."

What do you get if you pour boiling water down a rabbit hole?
Hot cross bunnies.

What do you get if you cross a potato with an onion?
A spud with watery eyes.

How do you cook toast in the jungle?
Under a gorilla.

"Have you heard the joke about the eggs?"
"No."
"Two bad."

What do you get it you cross a hyena with an Oxo cube?
An animal that makes a laughing stock of itself.

Mum: Don't you know it's rude to reach out for the cakes? Haven't you got a tongue?
Girl: *Yes, but my arms are longer.*

How do you make a potato puff?
Chase it round the garden.

What vegetable should you pick to go with jacket potatoes?
Button mushrooms.

What has twenty-two legs and goes crunch crunch crunch?
A football team eating crisps.

What jam can't you eat?
Traffic jam.

Waiter, this meal is terrible. Call the manager.
—*He won't eat it either, Sir.*

Waiter, what's wrong with this fish?
—*Long time, no sea.*

Waiter, what's this fly doing in my alphabet soup?
—*I expect he's learning to read.*

Waiter, this tea tastes like dishwater.
    —*Drink dishwater often, do we Sir?*

Waiter, there's a fly in my soup.
    —*Don't worry Sir, he won't drink much.*

Waiter, you've brought me the wrong order.
    —*Well you said you wanted something different.*

Waiter, this bun tastes of soap.
    —*That's right Sir, it's a bath bun.*

Waiter, do I have to sit here until I die of starvation?
    —*No Sir, we close at seven.*

Waiter, these eggs are bad.
    —*Don't blame me Sir, I only laid the table.*

Waiter, this soup tastes funny.
   —So, why aren't you laughing?

Waiter, there's a dead fly in my soup.
   —What do you expect for 50¢, a live one?

Waiter, you're not fit to serve a pig!
   —I'm doing my best, Sir.

Waiter, what's this in my soup?
   —I don't know Sir, all these insects look the same to me.

Waiter, why has this lobster only got one claw?
   —It was in a fight.
Well, take it away and bring me the winner.

Waiter, can I have some undercooked chips, cold beans, and a fried egg coated in grease?
　—*I'm sorry Sir, we couldn't possibly give you anything like that.*
Why not? You did yesterday.

Waiter, your tie is in my soup
　—*That's all right Sir, it's unshrinkable.*

Waiter, there's a flea in my soup.
　—*I'll tell him to hop it.*

Waiter, why is my food all mushed up?
　—*You did ask me to step on it.*

Waiter, are you in the Union?
　—*Yes Sir, I'm the chop steward.*

Waiter, is there soup on the menu?
　—*No Sir, I wiped it off.*

Waiter, there's a dead fly in my wine.
   —*Well you did ask for something with a little body in it.*

Waiter, I've only got one piece of meat.
   —*Hang on Sir, I'll cut it in two for you.*

Waiter, bring me a crocodile sandwich, and make it snappy.

How do you start a jelly race?
   Get set.

What car is like a sausage?
   An old banger.

What's bright yellow and dangerous?
   Shark-infested custard.

There was a man who had a blancmange in one ear and a jelly in the other.
He was a trifle deaf.

Why is a banana skin like a pullover?
Because it's easy to slip on.

What did the grape say when the elephant trod on it?
It just gave a little wine.

What does a vegetarian cannibal eat?
Swedes.

Why do bakers work so hard?
Because they knead the dough.

What stays hot in the fridge?
Mustard.

Man: I want six slices of bacon, and make them lean.
Butcher: *Certainly, sir. Which way?*

What flies and wobbles?
  A jellycopter.

Why are cooks cruel?
  Because they beat eggs, whip cream, and batter fish.

Why do people never starve in the desert?
  Because of the sand-which-is-there.

If you get a referee in boxing, a referee in rugby, and a referee in football, what do you get in bowls?
  Soup.

What sort of fish do cobblers prefer?
  Sole.

How can you tell that a wedding cake is sad?
Because of its tiers.

What sort of meat do karate experts prefer?
Chops.

What has knobs on and wobbles?
Jellyvision.

When is soup musical?
When it's piping hot.

Why did the elephant sit on the tomato?
It wanted to play squash.

What type of cake do children dislike?
A cake of soap.

A woman woke her husband up and said, "There's a burglar in the kitchen eating the cake I made this afternoon. Ring 000!"
"Who shall I ask for?" said her husband, "police or ambulance?"

How do you start a pudding race?
   Sago.

What do ghosts eat for supper?
   Ghoulash.

Eat up your spinach, It'll put colour in your cheeks.
   —*Who wants green cheeks?*

Mum, there's a black cat in the kitchen.
   —*That's all right, black cats are lucky.*
Not this one, he's just eaten Dad's dinner.

What is the difference between a young lady and a fresh loaf?
One is a well-bred maid and the other is well-made bread.

My dad is such a bad cook he even burns salad.

What is the fastest vegetable?
A runner bean.

Why does the apple tree cry?
Because people always pick on it.

What's green, covered in custard, and miserable?
Apple grumble.

What is round, red and cheeky?
Tomato sauce.

What do witches have for breakfast?
   Snap cackle and pop.

What do you get if you cross a cow with a duck?
   Cream quackers.

How can you tell when an elephant's been in the fridge?
   By the footprints in the butter.

What's short and green and goes camping?
   A boy sprout.

What vegetables do plumbers fix?
   Leeks.

What happened when there was a fight in the fish shop?
   Two fish got battered.

What's the best butter in the world?
A goat.

Why was the Egyptian pharaoh so sad?
Because he thought he'd lost his mummy.

Where does a vampire keep his savings?
In a blood bank.

Who's a vampire's worst enemy?
Mr. Tooth Decay.

What do you call a small child who won't make up his mind?
A maybe baby.

What do you call a layabout who's been caught in the rain?
A damp tramp.

What do you call a bird who lives around cows?
A dairy canary.

What do you call a stupid ruler?
A ding-a-ling-king.

What do you call a bloody yarn?
A gory story.

What do you call a giant fish at half price?
A whale sale.

What do you call a breakfast food for spirits?
Ghosties Toasties.

What do you call a ghost on crutches?
A hobblin' goblin.

What do you call a tired tent?
A sleepy teepee.

What do you call a wet seal?
  A damp stamp.

What do you call an insane flower?
  A crazy daisy.

What do you call a fake horse?
  A phony pony.

What do you call a fortunate water-bird?
  A lucky duckie.

What do you call arithmetic trails?
  Maths paths.

What do you call an insect's car?
  A roach coach.

What do you call a nasty bug that eats up the poor farmer's cotton?
  An evil weevil.

What do you call a witch's suitcase?
A hag bag.

What do you call a conversation between two large birds?
Stork talk.

What do you call a 747 puppy?
A jet pet.

What happens when the human body is completely submerged in water?
The telephone rings.

How can you make trousers last?
Make the coat and vest first.

Why is a bell the most obedient thing in the world?
Because it never speaks until it's tolled.

What do you have when you collect 100 female pigs and 100 male deer?
Two hundred sows and bucks.

What's the difference between a prize fighter and a person with a bad cold?
One knows his blows and the other blows his nose.

Why did the moth eat a hole in the rug?
Because it wanted to see the floor show.

What does a worm do in a cornfield?
It goes in one ear and out the other.

How can you make a slow horse fast?
Stop feeding him.

On which side does an eagle have the most feathers?
The outside.

What is it that is always behind the time?
The back of a clock.

What's grey, has two wheels, and weighs four tonnes?
An elephant on a motorcycle.

How does an elephant get out of a Volkswagen?
The same way he got in.

Why did the bald man buy a rabbit farm?
Because he wanted to grow some hares.

Why did the little dog almost itch to death?
Because he was so gentle that he wouldn't hurt a flea.

What do you call it when the members of an orchestra go on social security?
Band-aid.

Why is a kiss like gossip?
  Because it goes from mouth to mouth.

How can you tell if a cat burglar has been in your house?
  Your cat will be missing.

What do you call a duck physician?
  A quack doctor.

What do you call a slim parrot?
  Polly-unsaturated.

What did the topsoil say to the thunderstorm?
  "If this keeps up, my name will be mud!"

Where do moles go to get married?
  To the tunnel of love.

Why did the bus driver go broke?
Because he drove all of his customers away.

What did the stereo say to the record?
"Hi baby. How about going for a spin?"

If a man married a princess, what would he be?
Her husband.

What's the difference between an excited skunk and a calm skunk?
A twenty-dollar laundry bill.

What does Santa Claus say when he works in the garden?
"Hoe-Hoe-Hoe!"

When were the Dark Ages?
During the days of the knights.

Who was the famous chicken who rode with the Rough Riders and later became President?
Teddy Roostervelt.

Why do buffaloes always travel in herds?
Because they are afraid of getting mugged by elephants.

Why did Sir Lancelot take a torch into his bedroom?
Because he was afraid to sleep without a knight light on.

Where do fish keep their life savings?
In a river bank.

Who fights crime, eats bread crumbs, and has a secret identity?
Bat Mouse and Robin, the bird wonder.

What runs around the garden, keeps strangers away from your house, and has five hundred teeth?
A picket fence.

Where do sharks do their shopping?
At fish markets.

What do you call the autobiography of a shark?
A fishy story.

Why do baby birds never smile?
Would you smile if your mother fed you worms for dinner every night?

What did the rabbit give his girlfriend when he proposed to her?
A 24-carrot ring.

If Mounties always get their man, what do postmen always get?
Their mail.

Why do hummingbirds hum?
Because they can't remember the words.

How can you tell if an elephant is a mugger?
He'll be wearing a balaclava and hiding in a dark alley.

Why are giraffes good friends to have?
Because they're willing to stick their necks out.

Why do elephants have trunks?
Because they'd look silly wearing suitcases on their noses.

Good luck turns into bad luck when a rhino is chasing you and you find a nearby tree to climb... *only to find an ape in it.*

Good luck turns into bad luck when a neighbourhood layabout finally pays back the twenty dollars he owes you... *and the money turns out to be counterfeit.*

Good luck turns into bad luck when cockroaches evacuate your house... *only because termites are moving in.*

Good luck turns into bad luck when you call the credit card company to tell them they made a mistake on your bill... *and they agree with you only because they didn't charge you enough.*

Good luck turns into bad luck when you break a leg in front of a doctor's office... *and the doctor turns out to be an optician.*

Good luck turns into bad luck when lightning misses you and strikes a nearby tree... *and the tree falls on you.*

Good luck turns into bad luck when the handsomest boy in school calls you up... *and then apologises because he dialled the wrong number.*

Good luck turns into bad luck when you pick up a loose ball and run ninety metres for a try... *only to find out you ran the wrong way.*

Good luck turns into bad luck when it snows so much that you don't have to go to school... *and you end up spending the whole day shovelling the driveway and pavement.*

What is coq au vin?
A chicken on a lorry.

What's green and runs up the wall?
A runner bean.

What did the chef do when a customer fainted?
Gave her the quiche of life.

What did the dentist say when his wife baked a cake?
"Can I do the filling?"

What should you do for a starving cannibal?
Give him a hand.

What did one chick say to the other chick when it found an orange in their nest?
Look at the orange Mama laid.

What is woolly, covered in chocolate and goes round the sun?
A Mars Baaaa.

What do you get if you run over a canary with a lawn-mower?
Shredded tweet.

What go squeak-squeak when you pour milk over them?
Mice Crispies.

What cereal does an Eskimo have for breakfast?
Snowflakes.

What kind of person is fed up with people?
A cannibal.

Why are bananas never lonely?
Because they hang around in bunches.

Why did the woman get a shock when she picked up a bun?
The currant ran up her arm.

What is yellow and goes up and down?
A lemon in a lift.

"Two kilos of cats' meat please."
"Certainly Sir. Shall I wrap it or will you eat it here?"

What do you get if you put springs on a cow?
Milkshakes.

"Gran's cooking Sunday lunch for us."
"Yuk, I suppose that means Enthusiasm Soup again."
"What's Enthusiasm Soup?"
"She puts everything she's got into it."

What's sweet, white and fluffy, has whiskers, and floats?
A catameringue.

What do sea monsters eat?
Fish and ships.

What would happen if pigs could fly?
The price of bacon would go up.

What's the difference between here and there?
The letter T.

What do you serve, but never eat?
A tennis ball.

In what month do people talk the least?
February—because it's the shortest.

Why is a rabbit's nose always shiny?
Because she has her powder puff on the wrong end.

What has a foot at each end and a foot in the middle?
A yardstick.

Where did Noah keep his bees?
In the Ark hives.

What's white when it's dirty?
A blackboard.

What's the difference between a locomotive engineer and a school teacher?
One minds the train, and the other trains the mind.

Why did they put mirrors on chewing-gum machines?
So you can see what you look like when the chewing gum doesn't come out.

How many sides does a box have?
Two. The inside and the outside.

What do hippopotamuses have that no other animals have?
Baby hippopotamuses.

What bird can be heard at meals?
A swallow.

What's the best way to drive a baby buggy?
Tickle it's little feet.

How many big men were born in Sydney?
None. Only babies were born there.

When is it socially correct to serve milk in a saucer?
When you're feeding the cat.

What has one horn, runs up and down the street, and gives milk?
A milk truck.

How do you keep milk from turning sour?
Leave it inside the cow.

Which is faster—hot or cold?
Hot's faster. You can catch a cold.

What word is always pronounced wrong?
Wrong.

"Why aren't you the president of the mortgage department any more?"
"Well to tell the truth, I lost interest."

Bill: *Did you hear about the cross-eyed dog who chased a cat until it climbed out of reach?*
Will: No. What happened?
Bill: *The dog ended up barking up the wrong tree.*

Joe: Have you ever met the Invisible Man?
Moe: *No, but I hear he's out of sight!*

"Would you ever want to drive a taxi-cab for a living?"
   "No. I just couldn't hack the long hours."

A policeman who moonlights in rock bands as a drummer pounds a beat both day and night.

"How did you like the story about the Abominable Snowman?"
   "It left me cold."

Jerry: It's been a long day.
Perry: *It sure has. I've been up since the crack of yawn.*

Judy: *Your trousers look sad today.*
Rudy: What do you mean?
Judy: *Sort of depressed.*

What is the secret of success?
   "Push," said the doorbell.
   "Never be lead," said the pencil.
   "Take panes," said the window.
   "Always keep cool," said the ice.
   "Never lose your head," said the drum.
   "Make light of everything," said the fire.
   "Do a driving business," said the hammer.
   "Aspire to 'grater' things," said the nutmeg.
   "Be sharp in all your dealings," said the knife.
   "Find a good thing and stick to it," said the glue.

"What are the three words most often used by students?"
"I don't know."
"That's correct."

In school, they nicknamed me "Corns" because I'm always at the foot of my class.

Little Jimmy came home from his first day at school and told his mother he was never going back.
"What's the use of school?" he said. "I can't read and I can't write, and the teacher won't let me talk."

Jeff: Today, on the schoolbus, a little boy fell off his seat, and everybody laughed except me.
Teacher: *Who was the little boy?*
Jeff: Me.

Teacher: It you add 500, 391, 38, 162 and 17, then divide by 39 what would you get?
Lisa: *The wrong answer.*

Teacher: It you stood with your back to the north and faced due south, what would be on your left hand?
Davey: *Fingers.*

Band Student: Our high school orchestra played Beethoven last night.
Athlete: *Who won?*

Teacher: Oscar, if you had five pieces of candy, and Joey asked you for one, how many pieces would you have left?
Oscar: *Five.*

Teacher: Yes, what is it?
Failing Student: *I don't want to frighten you, but Dad said that if I don't get better grades someone's going to get a spanking.*

Teacher: Do you know why you make such poor grades?
Mortimer: *I can't think.*
Teacher: That's right.

Teacher: It's the law of gravity that keeps us from falling off the earth.
Silly Sally: *What kept us from falling off before the law was passed?*

Teacher: If I gave you two apples and told you to give one to your brother, would you give him the little one or the big one?
Ricky: *Do you mean my little brother or my big brother?*

Teacher: Name four animals that belong to the cat family.
Little Lena: *The mummy cat, the daddy cat and two kittens.*

Teacher: Now class, are there any questions?
Dizzy Lizzy: *Yes. Where do those words go when you rub them off the blackboard?*

Chemistry Teacher: What can you tell me about nitrates?
Cute Carol: *Well, I think they're cheaper than day rates.*

School Superintendent: Are they any unusual students in your class?
Teacher: *Yes—three of them have good manners.*

Teacher: What's usually used as a conductor of electricity?
Orville: *Why - er...*
Teacher: Correct, wire. Now tell me, what is the unit of electrical power?
Orville: *The what?*
Teacher: That's absolutely right. The watt.

Teacher: How do you spell Mississippi?
Small Sam: *The river or the state?*

When I was in school, I was the teacher's pet. She couldn't afford a dog.

Teacher: Charlie, can you define the system of checks and balances?
Charlie: *Sure, we have that in our family.*
Teacher: How do you mean?
Charlie: *I have the vote and dad has the veto.*